CRAFT TOPICS

INDIANS
OF THE PLAINS

FACTS • THINGS TO MAKE • ACTIVITIES

RUTH THOMSON

Franklin Watts
London • New York • Sydney • Toronto

© Franklin Watts 1991

First published in Great Britain
in 1991 by
Franklin Watts
96 Leonard Street
London EC2A 4RH

First published in the USA by
Franklin Watts Inc.
387 Park Avenue South
New York, N.Y. 10016

First published in Australia by
Franklin Watts
14 Mars Road
Lane Cove
NSW 2066

UK ISBN: 0 7496 0450 6

Editor: Hazel Poole
Text consultant: Dr. Colin Taylor
Designed by: Pinpoint Design
Artwork by: Chris Price
Photography by: Chris Fairclough
A CIP catalogue record for this book
is available from the British Library.

Printed in the United Kingdom

CONTENTS

U.S.S.R

Siberia

ARCTIC OCEAN

Greenland

Bering Strait

PACIFIC OCEAN

Tlingit

Haida

Nootka

Assiniboin

CANADA

Mandan

Iroquois

Sioux

UNITED

STATES

ATLANTIC OCEAN

Pomo

Navajo

Apache

Pueblo

Seminole

Key to Indian Territories

THE GREAT PLAINS

NORTH PACIFIC COAST

CALIFORNIA

SOUTHWEST

ESKIMO

NORTHERN PLAINS

WOODLAND

THE STORY OF INDIANS

Indians have lived in North America for thousands of years. Their ancestors came from Siberia, in Russia, over 20,000 years ago. They followed big game such as woolly mammoth and buffalo, crossing the shallow Bering Strait, which became a land bridge during the last Ice Age when the sea level dropped.

Gradually the Indians spread all over North, Central and South America and divided into different groups, or tribes, each of which developed distinct ways of life depending upon their environment.

▶ In the far north lived the Inuit, who hunted seal, walrus and polar bear. They travelled in boats made of stretched skin, called kayaks, and made snowhouses for shelter while hunting.

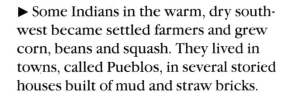

◀ On the damp, wooded Pacific coast, food, especially fish, was plentiful. The tribes there had time to develop arts and crafts and were renowned for their wood carving — in particular, for their totem poles.

▶ Some Indians in the warm, dry south-west became settled farmers and grew corn, beans and squash. They lived in towns, called Pueblos, in several storied houses built of mud and straw bricks.

◀ In the heart of America, where there were great, flat, windswept grasslands lived the Plains Indians. They were nomadic groups, constantly travelling in search of immense herds of buffalo which once roamed this land.

5

HUNTING BUFFALO

The Plains Indians depended upon the buffalo for their food, clothing and shelter. Buffalo are huge, lumbering creatures that used to live in herds of several thousand animals. If they were threatened in any way, they became very bad tempered and charged, so hunting them was both tiring and dangerous.

Before the hunters had horses, they followed the buffalo on foot. Up to 20 families went hunting together. They drove the buffalo through narrow canyons from which they could take good aim.

When Spanish explorers came to America, they brought horses with them. The Indians eventually caught wild horses and learned to tame and ride them. Their way of hunting changed.

▲ Sometimes they chased a herd over the edge of a cliff and collected the dead animals below.

In summer when the buffalo migrated in large numbers on the plains, lots of hunting bands gathered together. A chief led the tribes to the hunting grounds and organised the hunt with the leading men.

The bravest men were chosen as hunters. They had to follow strict rules. They were not allowed to go forward alone, or make any noises which might frighten away the herd. Anyone who did so was beaten and his personal things destroyed.

When a suitable herd was found, the hunters rode out on either side of it. As they gradually closed in, the frightened buffalo stampeded. The best horsemen galloped to the front of the herd and charged the leaders, so that they turned back. Other buffalo followed suit.

The hunters darted in and out among the confused buffalo, with their bows and arrows and spears. They aimed just behind the shoulder blades, so that the arrow would pierce the heart and kill the animal quickly. Even when the gun was introduced, the hunters preferred to use arrows because they found the guns too heavy and slow to reload.

The hunters chose horses that were fast and sure-footed and trained them to turn quickly. A pony learned to come level with a buffalo and then, at the touch of a knee, turn away as soon as the hunter had fired. The hunter leaned forward to aim, so it was important that the horse was trained not to shy away.

In the autumn, the bands hunted separately, moving camp when necessary to follow the buffalo. By November, they reached their winter camp, which was often in a sheltered river valley. In winter, blizzards, mist and icy winds made it difficult to hunt.

USING THE BUFFALO

After the buffalo were killed, each hunter identified the ones he had killed by the marks on his arrows. The women and children came to skin the animals and strip off the meat. Often, the brains and liver were eaten straightaway, to celebrate the success of the hunt. Sometimes, the hearts were left behind, since they were believed to have the power to restock the herd. Everything else was taken back to the camp. Not a single part of the buffalo was wasted.

The fresh meat was roasted on sticks or stewed with wild vegetables. The rest was cut into strips and dried on wooden frames in the sun. Some of the dried meat was pounded with berry stones and fat to make a nourishing food called pemmican and stored in rawhide envelopes, called parfleches, for winter use.

The buffalo hides had to be treated before they could be used. First they were soaked to loosen the hair and a few days later, stretched on a frame on the ground. All the fleshy parts, fat and hair were then scraped off. This work was done by the women.

The cleaned hides were rubbed with a mixture of brains and fat and then washed. Next they were softened by being pulled back and forth through a rope loop. Finally, they were stretched tightly on a wooden frame, laced to it by leather thongs, and left in a cool spot in the open air to dry slowly.

The Indians found a use for every part of the buffalo as well as its meat and hide.

▲ Hooves were boiled to make glue, fat was boiled to make soap and the dung was used as fuel. Even the tail came in useful as a fly whisk.

◄ Skins, with the hair left on, were used as blankets and as warm winter coats.

▲ The stomach lining was used as a water bucket.

◄ Outer robes, shoes and tipis were made from the skins.

▲ Babies were wrapped in soft skins and so were dead people for burial.

► The sinews were used for making bowstrings, as thread for sewing and as cord for tying arrowheads and feathers to arrow shafts.

► Horns were carved into spoons, powder flasks and rattles.

► The hair was twisted into rope, plaited into bridles or used for stuffing mattresses, saddles and lacrosse balls.

▲ Bones were made into hide-scrapers, knives, arrowheads, painting tools and even sledge runners.

9

LIVING IN A TIPI

Since the Plains Indians moved about so much, they lived in conical tents, called tipis. These could be put up and taken down quickly and were light enough for horses to haul. The covering was made of over a dozen buffalo skins sewn together into a semi-circle.

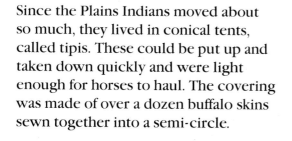

A tipi was hauled by a horse on a long wooden frame, called a travois.

The inside was lined with a dewcloth, made of decorated skins, which stopped water which ran down the poles from dripping into the inside of the tipi. The door generally faced east, towards the rising sun, and away from the west winds which swept the Plains.

Putting up a tipi was the work of two women. First, they made a cone-shaped frame of wooden poles and tied them with a rawhide cord.

The covering was tied to the top of the last pole to be put up and lifted into place.

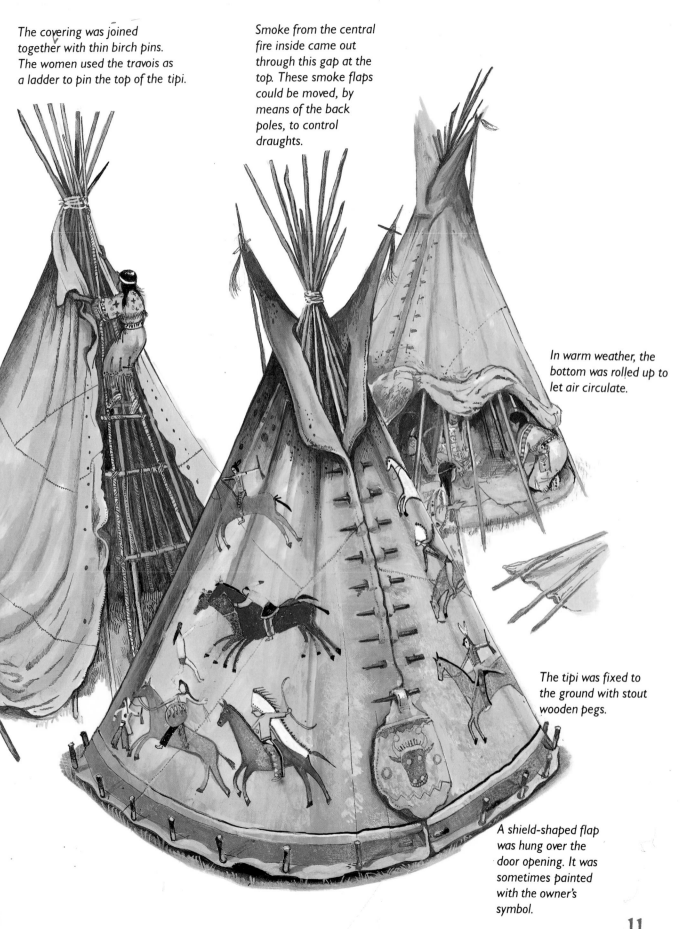

The covering was joined together with thin birch pins. The women used the travois as a ladder to pin the top of the tipi.

Smoke from the central fire inside came out through this gap at the top. These smoke flaps could be moved, by means of the back poles, to control draughts.

In warm weather, the bottom was rolled up to let air circulate.

The tipi was fixed to the ground with stout wooden pegs.

A shield-shaped flap was hung over the door opening. It was sometimes painted with the owner's symbol.

11

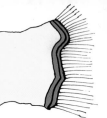

MAKING A TIPI

The shape of a tipi covering is a large semi-circle with two small semi-circles cut into it for the door opening and two smoke flaps. You can make it any size you like. Cut it out of either stiff paper or fabric. Decorate it with shapes or a hunting scene.

You will need: stiff paper or fabric • 3 plant support sticks • sticky tape • string • felt-tip pens or crayons

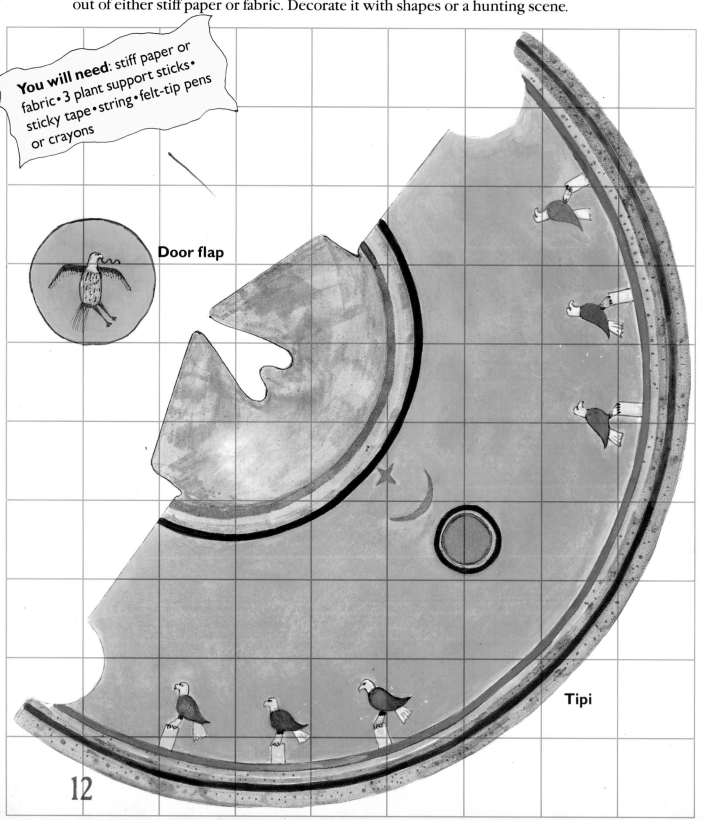

Door flap

Tipi

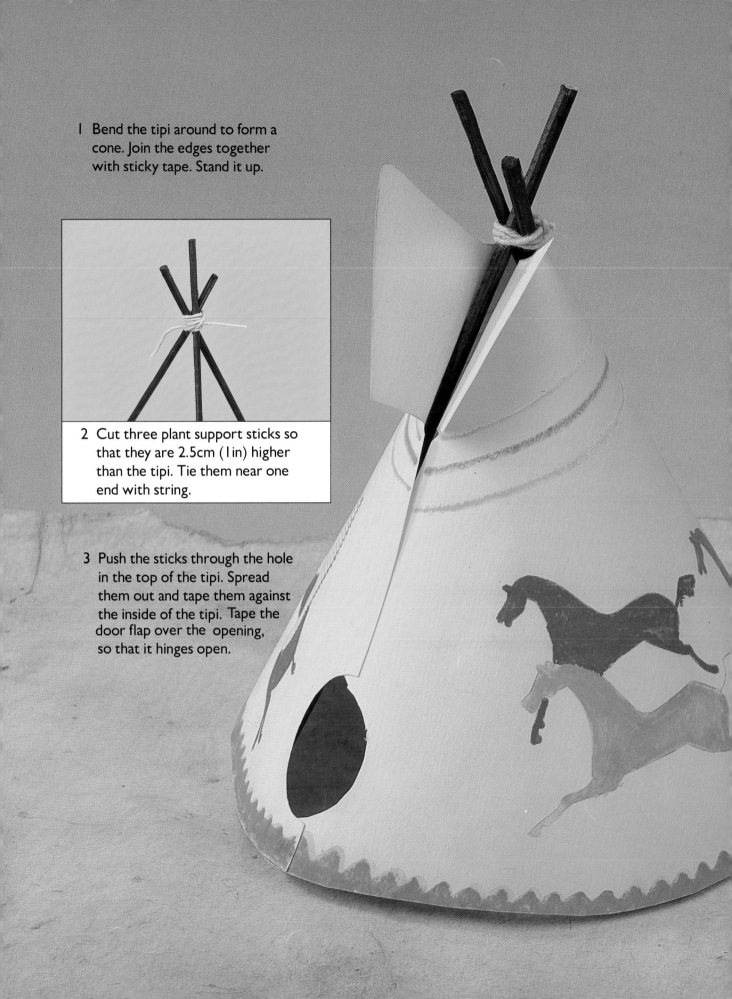

1 Bend the tipi around to form a
   cone. Join the edges together
   with sticky tape. Stand it up.

2 Cut three plant support sticks so
   that they are 2.5cm (1in) higher
   than the tipi. Tie them near one
   end with string.

3 Push the sticks through the hole
   in the top of the tipi. Spread
   them out and tape them against
   the inside of the tipi. Tape the
   door flap over the opening,
   so that it hinges open.

PICTURE WRITING

The Indians painted their tipis, war shields and ceremonial clothes with pictures. These were not simply for decoration. They were often symbols with magical or spiritual meanings or told stories in picture writing.

The tribal historians of the Sioux, for example, painted picture records on deerskin. These records were known as winter counts, because they marked the year between the first snowfall of one year and the next.

Each year was represented by symbols which stood for memorable events, such as a battle, good hunting, horse stealing, an eclipse, the killing of an enemy or disease.

The painters made brushes by chewing the end of willow or cottonwood twigs, or by tying deer hairs to the end of a stick. Sometimes they used the porous bones of animals. They used colours made from naturally coloured earths and plant stems and roots.

▲ Sam Kills Two, *a medicine man, is painting the symbol for 1926, the year a good agent left his reservation. This winter count shows 130 years of tribal history.*

SOME TYPICAL SYMBOLS

Thunderbird — a powerful spirit in the form of a huge bird. The Indians believed that the flapping of its wings made thunder and the flashing of its eyes made lightning.

The sun, the moon and stars — also considered to be very powerful spirits.

A warrior wearing his full war dress and bonnet, and carrying his shield and lance.

The buffalo — essential for the Plains Indians' survival and believed to have sacred powers.

Rain clouds

Deer

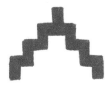

Mountains

Lightning

Bear Tracks

Bear

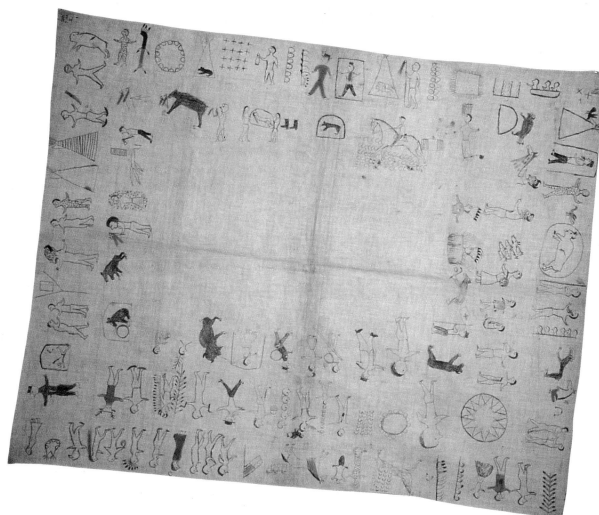

▲ Men painted stories of battles, dream dances or buffalo hunts.

See if you can draw a picture story about something important that has happened to you.

15

CLOTHES

Clothes were made from the skins of buffalo, moose, elk or deer. The women tanned the skins to make them soft and supple and sewed them together using an awl and buffalo sinew. Both men and women's clothes were highly decorated, usually with geometric patterns.

▶ *On ceremonial occasions, men wore a buckskin shirt. It was decorated with beads or quills. Some tribes trimmed their shirts with strips of fur or human hair to show they were very brave or important.*

▲ *In summer, men wore only a breechcloth, a long piece of soft buckskin that hung from a belt.*

▶ *Clothes and accessories were decorated with colourful beaded designs, as shown here. From left to right – a Sioux Indian's fringed leggings, women's leggings, blanket band, knife sheath, pipe bag and women's moccasins.*

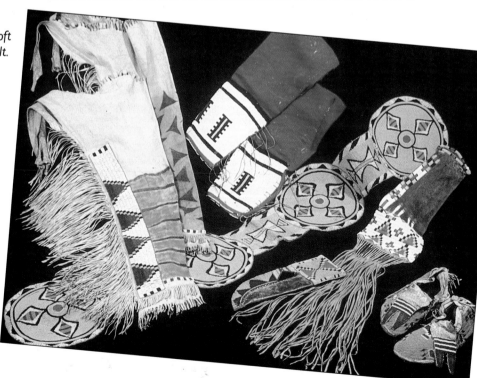

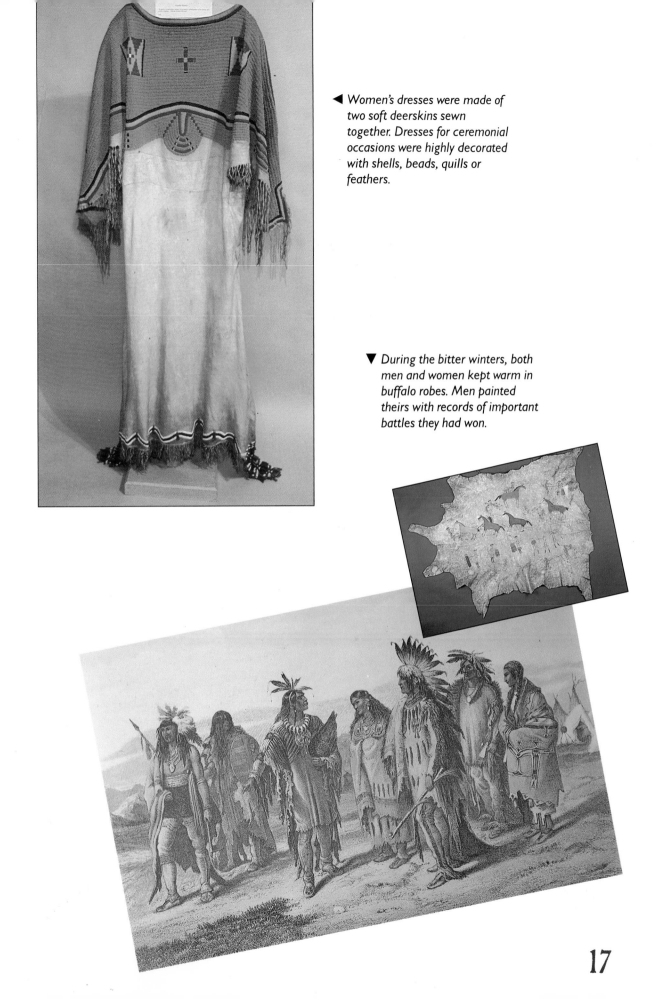

◀ Women's dresses were made of two soft deerskins sewn together. Dresses for ceremonial occasions were highly decorated with shells, beads, quills or feathers.

▼ During the bitter winters, both men and women kept warm in buffalo robes. Men painted theirs with records of important battles they had won.

MOCCASINS

Indians always wore soft-skin shoes called moccasins. Each tribe had its own design and decorations. Some moccasins were made from a single piece of leather and some had hard, rawhide soles. They were sewn with thread made from buffalo sinew and decorated with beads or porcupine quills. Moccasins were not very hardwearing, so Indians always took several pairs with them on long hunting or raiding expeditions.

Make your own moccasins out of thick felt.

You will need: thick felt • paper • pencil • scissors • pins • needle and cotton • beads (optional)

1. Fold a piece of paper in half. Put your foot on it, 1cm from the fold and 2.5cm from the bottom of the paper, and draw around your foot.

2. Take your foot away and draw another line for the moccasin shape. Start at the fold, follow 1cm away from the toes and then draw a straight line to the edge of the paper.

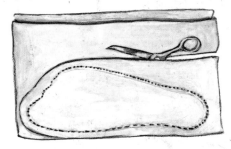

▲ *These porcupine quilled moccasins were made by Sioux Indians in about 1895.*

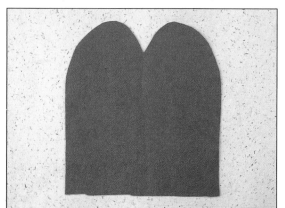

3. Open out your paper pattern and pin it flat on to the felt. Cut it out. Then turn the pattern over, pin it to the felt again and cut out a second shoe.

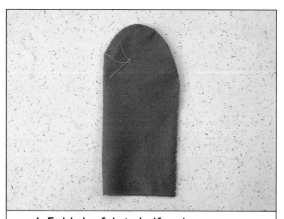

4. Fold the felt in half and overstitch it together, starting at the fold.

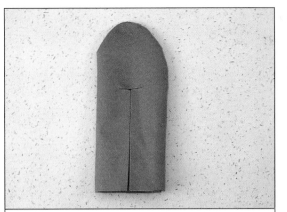

5. Turn the moccasin the right side out. On the top surface, cut an opening like this.

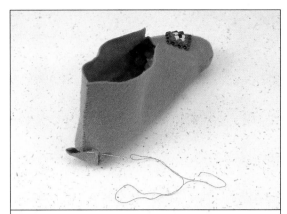

7. Sew the seam down the back of the heel first and then sew up the flap. Sew both seams on the outside.

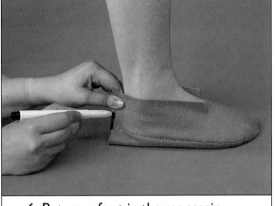

6. Put your foot in the moccasin and mark where your heel fits. Cut the felt, 1cm beyond your mark, following the curve. Cut a 2cm slit near the bottom of the heel.

Decorate your moccasins by sewing on felt scraps or beads or with embroidery.

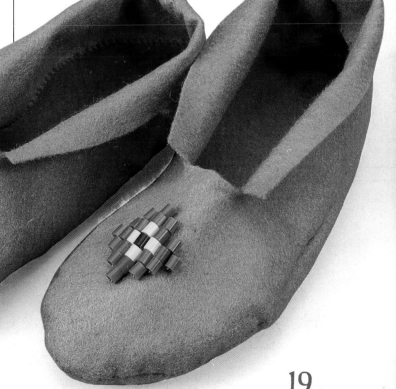

19

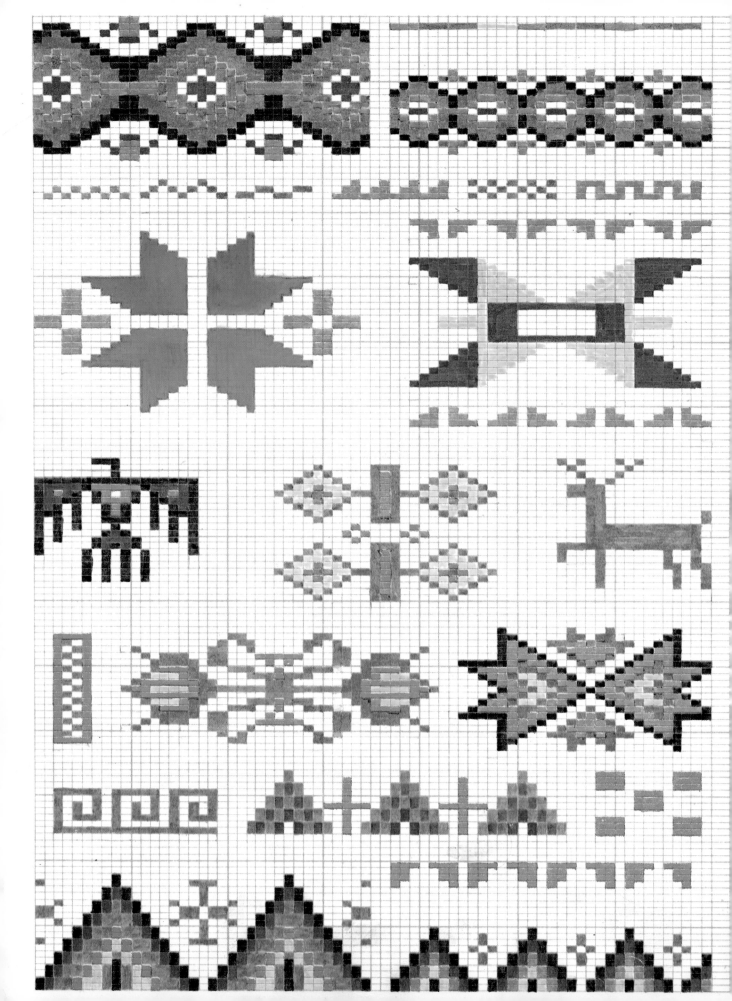

BEADWORK

Because they moved around so much, Plains Indians had few possessions and almost no ornaments or jewellery. Unlike settled tribes in other parts of North America, they did not make pottery or baskets, which would have been heavy or bulky to carry. Instead, they made most things from skins, which they always highly decorated. The Indians believed that making a skin beautiful honoured the spirit of the dead animal.

Before the arrival of the white man, the Indians used feathers, dyed porcupine quills or hair for decoration. In the 1800s, white traders brought coloured beads from Europe, which they gave to the Indians in exchange for animal hides. Each tribe developed its own beadwork patterns and colour combinations. These patterns were mainly abstract and geometric.

You will need: graph paper • felt pens or crayons • needle • strong thread • scissors • stiff fabric (for example, canvas) • coloured beads

◀ Try making patterns on graph paper, like those on the facing page. Choose a simple, repeating pattern to follow.

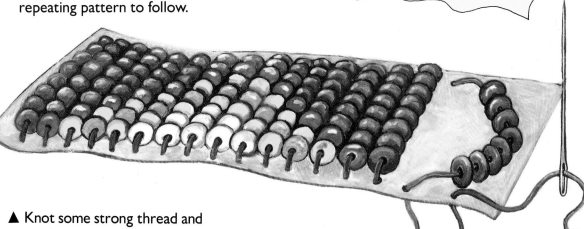

▲ Knot some strong thread and stitch it on to some stiff fabric, such as canvas, to hold it in place. String six or eight beads on to the thread and then stitch them down. Make a small stitch at the top of the next row of beads and repeat, following your pattern.

Beading was done only by women, who beaded virtually everything – clothes, moccasins, bags and cradleboards.

▲ A beaded saddlebag

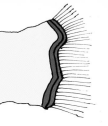

WARRIORS

Warfare was a constant part of Plains life. Tribes fought to defend their hunting lands, to capture horses and to show their strength. The men wanted to prove their daring as warriors, and their position in a tribe depended upon the success of their battle deeds.

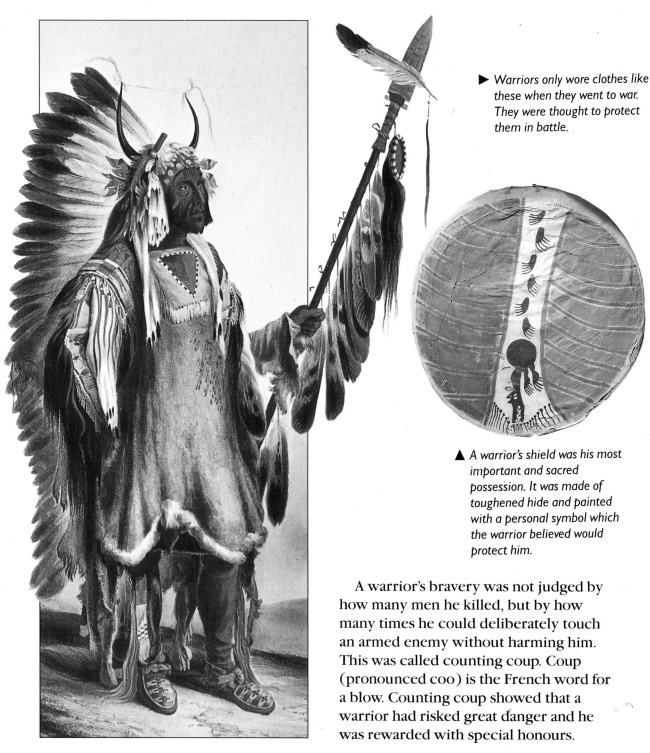

▶ Warriors only wore clothes like these when they went to war. They were thought to protect them in battle.

▲ A warrior's shield was his most important and sacred possession. It was made of toughened hide and painted with a personal symbol which the warrior believed would protect him.

A warrior's bravery was not judged by how many men he killed, but by how many times he could deliberately touch an armed enemy without harming him. This was called counting coup. Coup (pronounced coo) is the French word for a blow. Counting coup showed that a warrior had risked great danger and he was rewarded with special honours.

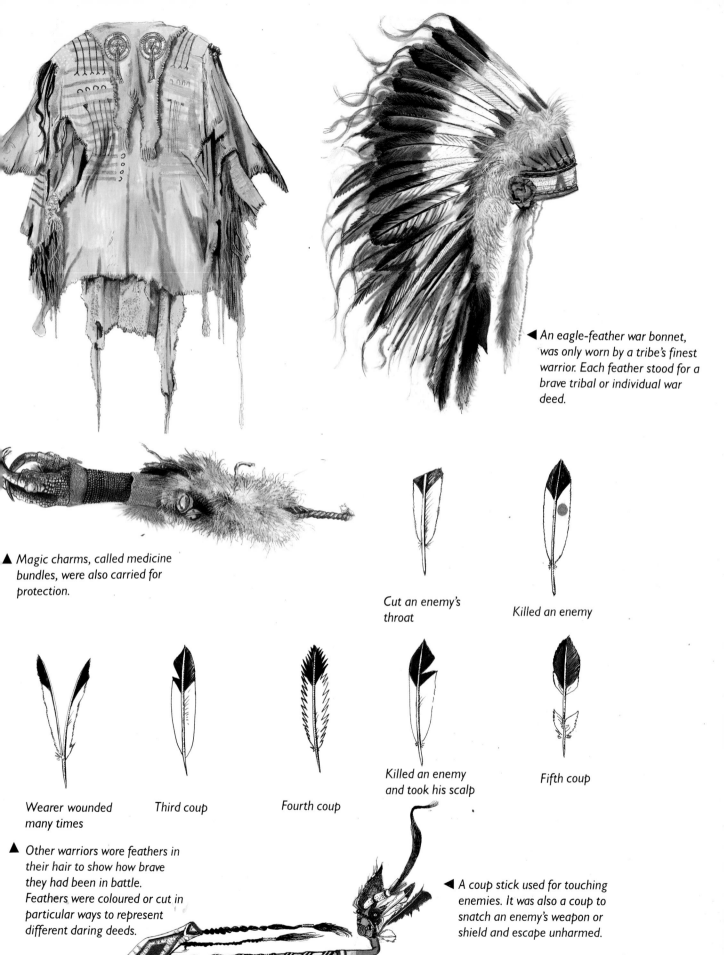

◀ An eagle-feather war bonnet, was only worn by a tribe's finest warrior. Each feather stood for a brave tribal or individual war deed.

▲ Magic charms, called medicine bundles, were also carried for protection.

Cut an enemy's throat

Killed an enemy

Wearer wounded many times

Third coup

Fourth coup

Killed an enemy and took his scalp

Fifth coup

▲ Other warriors wore feathers in their hair to show how brave they had been in battle. Feathers were coloured or cut in particular ways to represent different daring deeds.

◀ A coup stick used for touching enemies. It was also a coup to snatch an enemy's weapon or shield and escape unharmed.

23

MAKE A WAR BONNET

A war bonnet was made from the black-tipped tail feathers of an eagle. The eagle was considered the most sacred bird. It could fly the highest with its strong powerful wings, but had sharp sight to see everything that was happening on the ground. Ermine skins hung at the side of the bonnet. These were to give the warrior the skills of a weasel, known for its swift, fierce attacks and its ability to escape from enemies.

You will need: stiff paper • pencil • scissors • black paint • paintbrush • felt (assorted colours, including red and white) • embroidery thread • corrugated card (or thick elastic or webbing) • needle • cotton • white cotton fabric (optional)

MAKING THE FEATHERS

1 Cut strips of stiff paper about 20cm long and 8cm wide. Fold each one in half. Draw *half* a feather shape on the paper, with the centre on the fold.

2 Cut the feather shape out.

3 Open the feather out. Make diagonal snips all the way round it, except on the shaft.

4 Paint the top third of each feather black to look like an eagle feather.

5 Cut small squares of red felt. Fold the shaft of the feather and wrap the felt around it, tucking the ends inside the fold.

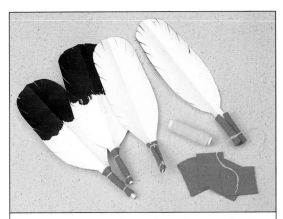

6 Tie embroidery thread around the felt to hold it in place and knot it at the back.

MAKING THE BONNET

1 Cut a length of corrugated card, thick elastic or webbing, long enough to fit around your head.

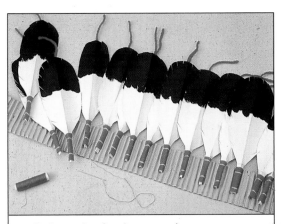

2 Sew the feathers to the headband at regular intervals.

MAKING THE ROSETTES

1 Cut a circle of felt, about 5cm in diameter. Cut two smaller circles, in contrasting colours, one slightly smaller than the other.

2 Put them one on top of the other in order of size, with the biggest one on the bottom. Stitch them together through the centre and then stitch them to the sides of your war bonnet.

Cut two strips of white felt or cotton fabric for the ermine strips and stitch them in place under the rosettes.

SIGN LANGUAGE

The Plains tribes all spoke different languages. However, they could communicate with one another by using hand signs, rather like deaf people do. Learn some of these signs and see if you can have a conversation with a friend. You might like to invent some new signs of your own for modern words, such as television, computer or skateboard.

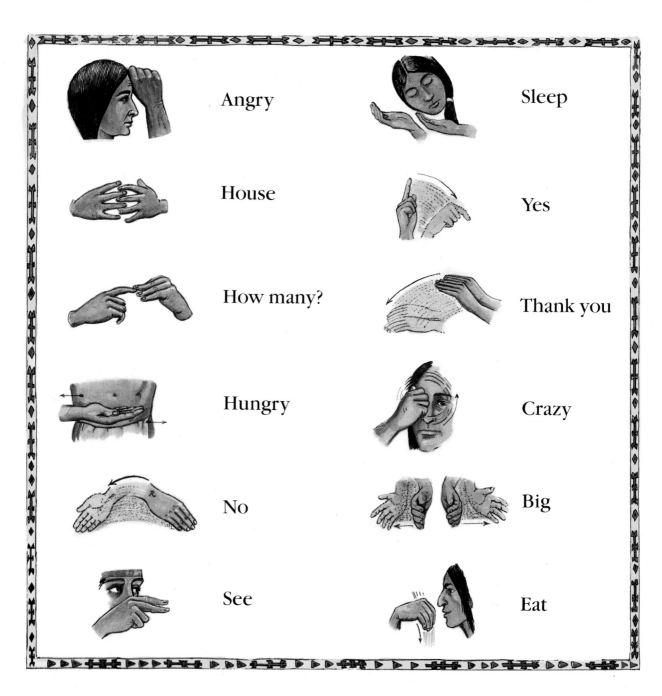

Angry

Sleep

House

Yes

How many?

Thank you

Hungry

Crazy

No

Big

See

Eat

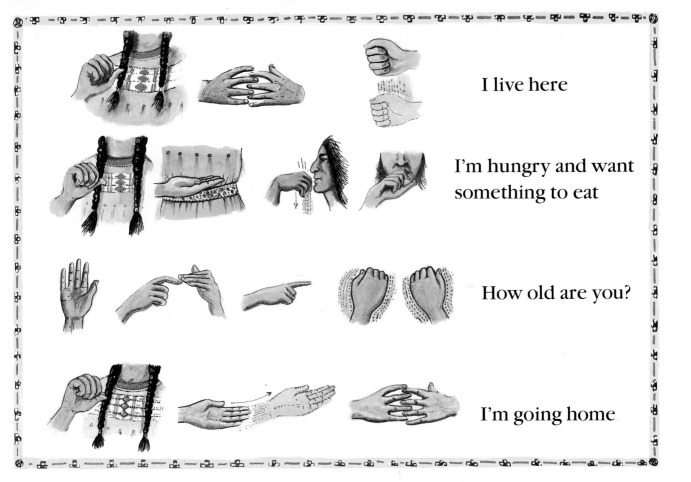

I live here

I'm hungry and want something to eat

How old are you?

I'm going home

When hunters went out for several days, they sometimes left a trail for others to follow. They used whatever natural materials they found along the way, such as grass, twigs or stones.

▼ *Make a trail, using these signs, in your local park or woods and see if other people can follow it.*

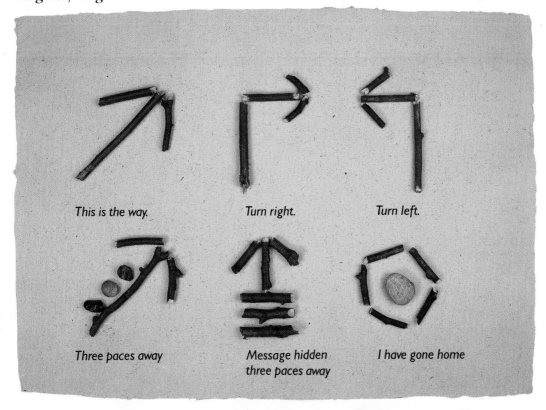

This is the way.

Turn right.

Turn left.

Three paces away

Message hidden three paces away

I have gone home

27

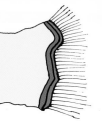

DID YOU KNOW?

Why are the Indians so called?

In 1492, Christopher Columbus set off from Spain to discover a sea route to Asia. When his ships sighted land, six weeks later, he mistakenly thought he had sailed all the way round the world and reached a group of islands off the coast of Asia.

He called the people he met on San Salvador, the first island he landed upon, "los Indios", meaning Indians. In fact, of course, Columbus had reached America, not Asia at all, but his name for the native people of America stuck.

What Columbus did not discover was that there were hundreds of groups of people scattered across America, each with their own distinctive name, language and customs.

What's the difference between a tipi and a wigwam?

A tipi is a hide-covered, conical tent in which the Plains Indians lived. The word *tipi* simply means dwelling. A wigwam is a birch bark or rush-mat covered hut that the Woodland Indians built. Both are built with poles. Tipis have long poles which tie at the top. Wigwams have poles which are bent over.

Are there still herds of buffalo on the plains?

In the early 1800s, it was estimated that there were as many as sixty million buffalo roaming the plains. But as white men came westwards across the plains, looking for farmland, building railroads and on the trail for gold in California, they began slaughtering the buffalo. Hunters were employed to kill buffalo to feed the thousands of railroad workers. Hide dealers killed millions more for their skins, which proved good for making fine leather. Once the railroad was built, it became a popular sport to shoot buffalo through the train windows. By 1889, there were only 541 buffalo left. Today, protected herds live in American National Parks.

Tipi

Wigwam

How did Plains Indians send smoke signals?

Indians sent smoke signals to tell each other that there were enemies about. They built fires on mountain ledges overlooking wide plains where the smoke would be easily seen. The fires were lit under a pyramid of branches.

Once a fire was blazing, it was smothered with damp grass and a blanket thrown over it. To send a message, the blanket was quickly removed and a balloon-shaped puff of smoke would rise into the air. The blanket was replaced and removed at regular intervals to make a coded message in puffs of smoke. On a clear day, the smoke could be seen from great distances.

Why did Indians paint their faces?

Paint had a sacred or magical meaning. Indians painted their faces either to frighten away evil spirits and enemies, to give them magic powers for hunting or for war, or to show their position in a tribe. When the Indians did ceremonial dances, they painted themselves with patterns particular to each dance.

The colours did not represent exactly the same thing in every tribe, but usually red meant war, white meant peace and purity and black meant death. Yellow was for either joy or bravery and blue meant defeat or other kinds of sadness.

Since paint was considered magical, it was kept safely in buckskin bags. It was mixed with buffalo grease before use, so that it was smooth to apply.

What are the names of the Plains Indian tribes?

There were several dozen different tribes which lived on the Plains. The tribes which were completely nomadic and lived in the way this book describes were:

Arapaho
Assiniboin
Blackfoot
Cheyenne
Comanche
Crow
Gros Ventres
Kiowa
Teton Sioux

GLOSSARY

Awl A pointed tool used for making holes.

Coup An Indian war honour. It was considered far braver to touch an enemy with either a hand, weapon or *coup stick* and escape unharmed, than to kill him.

Cradleboard A wooden frame covered with leather skin, which a mother used for carrying her baby on her back.

Lacrosse A team game, similar to hockey. Players have sticks with nets to catch the ball and score by getting the ball into their opponents' goal.

Parfleche A large rawhide wallet used for carrying dried food.

Plains The area that lies between the Rocky Mountains in the west and the Mississippi river in the east and which stretches from Texas up to Canada. It is mostly grassland.

Rawhide An animal skin that has not been softened by tanning.

Reservation Land which has been set aside for exclusive use by Indians.

Sinew The tissue which joins a muscle to a bone.

Tanning The soaking treatment of animal hides to soften and turn them into leather.

Travois An A-shaped wooden frame with two long poles on which first dogs, and later horses, pulled an Indian family's belongings.

War bonnet A warrior's feathered head-dress.

RESOURCES

John Judkyn Memorial,
Freshford Manor, Freshford,
Nr Bath
Tel: 0221 223312

A collection of circulating exhibits and loan kits, including materials on American Indians, available to schools.

Public House Bookshop,
21 Little Preston Street,
Brighton, BN1 2HQ

This bookshop specialises in books on native Americans.

Twinlight Trail,
2 Buckingham Lodge,
2 Muswell Hill, London N10 3TG
Tel: 081 444 5436

This organisation holds a regular programme of craft fairs throughout the year, selling authentic Indian artefacts, jewellery and books. It also has a comprehensive list of books, cassettes, albums and pictures which can be bought by mail order. Send a large SAE for details.

PLACES TO VISIT

The American Museum in Britain,
Claverton Manor, Bath BA2 7BD
Tel: 0225 63538

The museum is open from Mar 28 – November 2, from Tuesday to Sunday, 2 – 5. There is a gallery devoted to American Indians and a replica of a tipi in the grounds. The museum also has publications about the native people of North America available by post. Send an SAE for a book list.

City of Bristol Museums and Art Gallery,
Queen's Road, Bristol BS8 1RL
Tel: 0272 299771

The museum is open from Monday to Saturday, 10 – 5. It has a small collection of Plains Indian material, especially costumes.

Hastings Museum and Art Gallery,
Johns Place, Cambridge Road, Hastings, East Sussex TN34 1ET
Tel: 0424 721202

The museum is open from Monday to Saturday, 10 – 1, 2 – 5 and Sunday from 3 – 5. The collection on display is related mainly to Sioux and Blackfoot Indians.

Horniman Museum,
London Road, Forest Hill,
London SE23 3PQ
Tel: 081 699 1872

The museum is open from Monday to Saturday, 10.30 – 6 and Sunday 2 – 6. It has ethnographical collections from all parts of the world, including North America.

Museum of Mankind,
Burlington Gardens,
London W1X 2EX
Tel: 071 437 2224

The museum is open from Monday to Saturday, 10 – 5 and Sunday 2.30 – 6. It contains some Plains Indians artefacts in the display introducing visitors to its collection. It also has a small bookshop and a reference library open to the public in the afternoons.

Pitt Rivers Museum and Department of Ethnology and Prehistory,
South Parks Road,
Oxford OX1 3PP
Tel: 0865 270927

The museum is open from Monday to Saturday, 1 – 4.30. Phone to enquire about opening times on public holidays.

Royal Museum of Scotland,
Chambers Street,
Edinburgh EH1 1JF
Tel: 031 225 7534

The museum is open from Monday to Saturday, 10 – 5 and Sunday 2 – 5. It has a small collection of Plains Indian material on display, including clothing, weapons and domestic equipment.

University Museum of Archaeology and Anthropology,
Downing Street,
Cambridge CB2 3DZ
Tel: 0223 337733

The museum is open from Monday to Friday, 2 – 4, and Saturday 10 – 12.30. It has a good collection of Plains Indian material.

INDEX